Stones in the Stream

Stones in the Stream

A collection of Poems
by
Tricia Heriz-Smith

Poet in Residence Press

England, South Africa, Germany, Italy

Bibliographic information of the German National Library:
the German National Library (Deutsche Nationalbibliothek)
catalogs this publication in the German National Bibliography
(Deutsche Nationalbibliografie).

Detailed bibliographic information can be found
on the internet website: http://dnb.ddb.de.

Produced and published in Germany by:
BoD – Books on Demand, Norderstedt, Germany.

ISBN: 978-3-7519-2425-2

Cover image 'Zen stones balance' by Kaz of Pixabay

Acknowledgements

This book has been many years in the writing, long before I even conceived of it as a book. The fact that it has birthed now is largely due to Diana Button and the Poets in Residence group, Nada Kojic-Edwards, Sanford Clark, Jennifer Rundle, whose varied voices taught me to trust my own.

Over the past decade, Diana Button has been my poetic companion, inspiring me to go deeper and to keep writing. Apart from all her practical help without which these poems would never have made it to a computer let alone been published, her encouragement has been a constant beacon towards finding and valuing my own creative voice. I cannot thank you enough.

There are many people who have been a part of my creative life at different times. Some have remained close, and others have taken different paths, yet all of them have contributed in one way or another, often unconsciously. Long before I took myself seriously as a writer and poet, Cliff Penwell encouraged me to give my muse, Rabbit, a voice. Louise Broomberg welcomed my Attunement Poems and Miriam Platt, a sister poet, taught me to value the inspiration that arose. Thank you all, and others in my EDL years who encouraged me to look below the surface and to seek inspiration.

Showing poems to family and friends is always daunting, and I appreciate how my daughter, Zilla Pearse, has been so willing to listen to poems at times when she has had many other things on her mind, and to her and Kurt Unger for inviting me to write poems as presents for friends. It meant so much to me to be asked to do this. Thank you.

Most of the early poems were saved by my daughter, Tanya Gazet du Chattelier, who provide house room for my old journals when I moved to Italy. I know it was annoying, especially as you were moving home yourself, but thank you.

My mother, Joan Robinson, who features in these poems by her nickname "Tiger", and who always took the road less travelled encouraging me to do the same, thank you for your courage and love. Both you and my father, Alan Graham-Smith, brought me up to believe in the importance of being creative, original and true to myself. It must have been difficult for you and I appreciate that you were always there for me.

And you, my readers, as you dip into this book and its varied poems, I hope you will find some that speak to you. I am honoured that you should take the time to read them and hope that they will give you pleasure and stimulate new thoughts, Sharing poetry is a very intimate experience and I appreciate your willingness to walk along this stream with me and participate in this conversation.

we are all stones
connected one to another
without you, silence

To my family
both present, past and future
this, I dedicate to you

Contents

Foreword

Stones in the Stream, the life-work of Tricia Heriz-Smith, is a beautiful collection of poems from a lifetime of practicing deep living and the writing life. Tricia gifts us with a book filled with astute observations, explorations and invitations to look deeply into this world of ours and to familiarise ourselves with things that are at one and the same time, evidence of our many differences, our uniqueness and our sameness.

Tricia's concern for the world, for equality, for justice, for political correctness and for a felt sense of belonging comes across with clarity and touches the reader in all the right places. Her work undoubtedly draws on a life of experience and movement in and out of differing cultures and countries including South Africa, United Kingdom, Italy, Germany and Malaysia.

This collection shows us our mirror image like water does our face, inviting us to look again at our fixed ideas and points of view.

Our common humanity, our shared responsibility are important themes that re-emerge and connect through and across the chapters of her book as it runs its course towards the open sea. Each poem - each stone – has the potential to grab us and pull us into the current and stream that is converging into one flow.

Tricia's keen eye for detail, her ability to observe the familiar and to then reveal this to the reader in a new light is an open invitation to enter into this dance with life, into other voices, other perspectives and have the courage to look through the eyes of the unfamiliar other: eyes that have the potential to transform.

When I asked Tricia what function poetry has in her life, for her personally and for the world at large, she offered some beautiful responses that I would like to share here with you:

> *Poetry has the power to make impossible connections that remove blinkers from my heart; it enables me to be present in a deeply conscious way and at the same time connected with some universal underlying energy and then to be able to lift this into concrete form.*

Poetry, and particularly writing poems, are a way to connect with a deep understanding, a way of looking at the world around and really seeing it, and trying to share that perception, firstly with myself over time and then (now) with others.

I suppose that in many ways, poetry is my spiritual practice, like (if not more than) meditation or yoga. The composition of poems is the place where I can dive deep and is a time of transcendence which fuels and energises the rest of my day. In some ways it is prayer at its essential essence. In writing poems I'm seeking a universal truth (god) that underlies everything, and looking for the metaphors / words to clarify that perception.

All I would like to add is a large and loud, thank you Tricia for this wonderful collection of poems. Through it, you have not only gifted us with your compassionate heart and voice, but have gifted yourself and others with poetry at its essence.

Preface

There is an art to standing on one leg just as there is to balancing one rock on another. Outer balance can only happen with inner balance, and that search has been mine for as long as I can remember.

These are poems of discovery, just as when you walk on a pebbly beach you find one stone calling to you to be picked up and taken home. Sometimes, several clamour at once for attention! I remember my brother-in-law, Ambrose Campbell, being overwhelmed by the stones on the beach at Aldeburgh, Suffolk in the 1960's, and filling bag after bag with stones to take back to London because they spoke to him.

So, these poems have been picked from moments in the stream of my life that have caught my full attention and demanded to be written.

seeking that centre
where all is in balance
withstand waves

This collection has come together at a time of great social upheaval as the Coronavirus challenges every country to handle this pandemic, and I was touched to see that China printed labels on the boxes of supplies they sent to Italy which read "we are waves from the same sea" (lines accredited to Seneca) to express their brotherhood in this extraordinary time. Poetry doesn't preach like prose, it can slip in and convey in a few syllables universal truths. It's an art of encapsulation and reduction. Poetry makes impossible connections that remove blinkers from my heart. Poetry enables me to be present in a deeply conscious way and at the same time connected with some universal underlying energy and then to be able to lift this into concrete form. They are word synchronicities, a form of magic.

For myself, the main motivation in writing is to better understand myself, my world and to connect with it at the deepest truth level possible. It is to shine a spotlight on an understanding condensed into its most concrete form in words. The poem is the synthesis of all this and the journey is an integral part and equally important.

My motivation for publishing? I suppose that this is in many ways my legacy! My children and grandchildren are the living breathing realities of who I am and have been, and have taken this to their own unique realms. My poems are the distillation of my own time and space, rather like messages in a bottle tossed into the stream of life. I suppose at some level I see them as my epitaph, my memorial! In this age when the tombstones and grave sites of our ancestors are less present in our well travelled world, they are my gift to the future and where I can be found by those who care to visit. And you don't even need to bring flowers!

For readers? I hope this will be an inspiration to you to acknowledge and find your own creative voice.

VARIOUS POEMS

each stone
balances one on another
- celebrate gravity

Abortion

I have a right to choose
for it's my life,
my creation,
yet you would stand
in the way and refuse.
You
who deny me life
beyond that of slavery,
who think
I have no place
but to serve your needs
and that my creativity
is less than yours,
my purpose
less meaningful,
my art
mere decoration.
And yet,
i am the one who bleeds,
who,
in the dead of night
awakes
to tend my creation,
who suffers for my love,
while you,
you simply take
what is not yours
and use me
like a fallow field
in which to impregnate
your ideas
until the weeds poison

and stifle
the true wheat of my being.
I weep for those
innocents
you kill for your pleasure,
those you ignore
and neglect
in your pride,
for the wasteful contradiction
of your existence,
and the destructiveness
of your power.
We are the same,
you and I,
though you deny me,
would I deny you?

Always drink upstream from the herd
-Will Rogers-

Rampling, trampling, rolling in mud,
the herd comes to the water's edge
churning, turning, moving about
they come to slake their thirst

Roiling, boiling, hot as a furnace
they sink up to their hocks
snorting, cavorting and playing around
they churn up all the ground

Hubbling, bubbling, over the rocks
clear water turns to brown
slipping, sliding into the mill
the herd here drinks its fill

Quietly, slowly, all alone
the leader stands on guard
watching, waiting, on alert
he moves towards the stream

Sparkling, gurgling, crystal clear
the water that he drinks
tumbling, rumbling down the stream
to where the herd awaits

Black and white

A figure moves across a hill -
just one I see
his white clothes loud against the green.
And then, for a moment
he's gone.

All is confusion.

Then, as he emerges,
his whiteness defines the outline of another
that only now is seen briefly
before he appears to walk on alone.

Two figures walking on a distant hill -
one so clear
the other obscure,
whose presence
from here,
is known solely by its impact on the world.

Two figures walking on a distant hill

#me too

Of course ...
given the gift of vibrant life,
the ugly and deformed
were always attracted.

Only power,
of money or position,
provided the courage
to encroach,
then –
if you had been vibrant yourself,
like to like,
maybe
you would not have been repulsed, repulsive

#me too

The weak can never forgive.
Forgiveness is the attribute of the strong.
- Ghandi -

Forgiveness, forgive me,
for I know not what I do,
I crave your kind forgiveness
for the things I plan to do.

If I was strong and able
and my heart was bold and stable
then I wouldn't be unable
to resist this kind of fable
from the political rabble
who seem to endlessly babble
while we follow like a gaggle
of geese to be slaughtered
and fed to the daughters
of the rich and famous
who feel shameless
and aimless
while thoughtlessly bleeding
the people their leading
who continue their breeding
providing more fools for the mills
to be killed without skills.

Must it always be such,
for I think it's too much
that you smarmily ask
and say it's our task
to forgive your sins
while continuing

to destroy and to break
our worth and our stake

and you ask us to make
a world that is fake
with no care and concern
and no fair return
for the effort we learn
that was wasted indeed
on your powerful needs.

A Carpet Tale

weave a life of contrasts
with strands of give
and take
interspersed with pearls
grown from the grit
of challenge
backed by strong canvas
of values you hold key

don't hang it on the wall
for all to marvel at its form
but lay it on the floor
a carpet for your friends
where feet will burnish it
and add an extra sheen
and cushion them from
stubbing toes on rocks
that lie unseen

and should you feel
alone and feared
and fall down on your knees
the warp and weft
of all you've been
will wrap your care around

and should you feel
too poor of soul
to struggle up once more
then gather up the priceless pearls

and hold them close to you
as symbols of past strengths

and should you feel
too fragile
to continue on your way
then know
that what you hold most dear
will anchor you
right here

After the Storm

The stillness
and the morning light
defies the fury
of the storm threshed night
Awaken
to an endless sight
from darkness
and a thunderous fright
And after the tempestuous trial
the fresh washed world
is full of smile
That cancels out the angry bile
with promises of peace awhile.

A Walk Together

Come, stroll with me.
it's early still,
and the dew sparkles on bent grasses
wetting our shoes
and leaving trace of our passing.

It's spring time,
And the scents assault us,
birds harangue us with hope
flowers crave the warmth and longer days
And all around new life clamours.

Your voice is muted in awe
of nature's story,
tuned in to this moment
watching the light iridescent
sparkle upon leaves.

I'm glad you joined me,
I whisper later,
forgetting what it was we meant to share,
but glad we now have
this brief memory, together.

A Woodland Song

In the bright sunlight of the meadow
tall poppies lift their heads
in exultation
shouting for attention.

Amidst the melting waters
fragile snowdrops peak
harbingers of Change.

In the deep forests
their essence assaults me,
hidden and shy,
the woodland violet,
over powers me
fragile and luminous
the carpet of bluebells,
is crushed underfoot.

In this, your kingdom,
in the half light,
I am afraid.
I blunder around,
and in my enthusiasm,
clumsily
destroy
that which is
so beautiful,
so delicate.

I imagine a vase,
full of woodland flowers,
sharing their beauty.

I would pluck your drooping head
and lift it to the sun,
but the truth is, once picked,
unlike the sunny rose,
you wilt and die
before I can even get you
home.

Dialogue

Let's talk
about the things
that matter
to you and I
and find a place
to hear
each other's words
resound
with new meaning
fresh carved
from our connection
to the each other.

I will hold my thoughts
of thou suspended
so as to let
your heart
guide my understanding
to a new place
and the words
take on a new vibration.

This
I can only do
when fired
by respect
for who you are
that equals
who I think I am
and opens up my ears

to listen deeply
beyond the noise

our voices make
to what the silence
would convey.

When
I can sit beside you
and hear your breath,
and feel your rhythm,
then,
and only then
will I be open to receive
thou.

Deep Play

Come,
let me invite you
into a place
where time moves
at its own pace and
not by some
invisible metronome
within your head.

Come,
take up the challenge to explore
beyond your comfort zone
to shed convention and
self absorption then
loose your constructed self.

Come,
face the danger
of stepping
out of the known and familiar
where friends will map
"here be dragons"

Come,
let yourself sink
into the present presence
transcendent
rapturous
ecstatic
fully now.

Come,
dive off the rock
of your certainties
into unchartered seas
of creativity
discover your wings

Come,
for this is deep play
it is the essence
of who we are
in our discoveries and creations

Come,
though you travel alone
for there is no other way
I'll meet you there
at the edge of eternity

Come,
for this is the secret
of the philosopher's stone
changing the base nature.

Distraction's Discord

So much time is spent in dis
traction, avoiding moments of dis
aster, keeping fear a dis
tant threat and far from me, dis
may at bay.

These thoughts arise from dis
mal lakes that in my heart I dis
approve, that come to frequently dis
turb my peace of mind in dis
array and stay.

How can I move from dis
illusion where linger these dis
jointed lies so that these demons in dis
grace no longer dwell but dis
appear from here

It is so easy to sink in dis
connection leaving a mind confused and dis
traught to drown in dis
combobulation or dwell in a dis
severed state forever.

Don't linger in this garden of dis
ease where it's impossible to dis
able the longing to dis
pose of feeling deep dis
pair - beware.

Dull

In or out?
It's so much easier
to receive than to give,
and so I stand,
creative urge swelling
and reach for my link
to the outside world
to drown out
the whisper of my gift
in the trumpet blast
of mindless fodder
for just a minute, until
an hour later,
I realise that I was dead
for that time
in meaningless space.

Dead to reality
in second hand emotions
that like a drug
dull the ache for life.

Edgar Allan Poe:

All that we see and seem
is but a dream within a dream
a construct of our thinking mind
that seeks to conquer and to bind
the threads of living into lines
that common sense can then define
as only this, or sometimes that
but never Schroeder's cat.

All that we see and seem
is but a dream within a dream
a picture formed like holographs
from tiny bits to those quite vast
that we will swear show all the tale
for we were never known to fail
at making two plus two become
far more than four in our sum.

All that we see and seem
is but a dream within a dream
a life prolonged beyond its time
would seem to us to be a sign
that we are better far than thee
for we have stored abundantly
and plundered without fear of cost
and can't believe that all is lost.

All that we see and seem
is but a dream within a dream
and now we near the end of time
we start to realise our crime

for we were figments of our minds
who left reality behind
to create fantasy and pain
that leaves upon this earth a stain.

Escape

Fear and longing flows through my veins
as in the rank darkness your dread fills my heart
700 bodies crammed in flight
sacrificing all for hope
seeking new life
being rocked to death.

The wind rises lifting my fear
beyond reason.
The turbulence sickens
stomachs already weak and starved.
The screams torment the mind
beyond enduring,
and still I hope and trust.

There is no going back
as I'm tossed forward.
Purged of all faith
I cling to you,
to harbour my own.
What now of the promise
of a better life?

If only I'd stayed,
not paid,

then maybe some, or one,
could have lived
beyond this time.

No time for thoughts,

regrets,
dreams.
All is lost in the cold, cold wash
of waters over my head.
Drenched by despair
I tumble,
clutching at ropes
that don't hold,
burn through my hands,
battered by spars
and the bodies of others,
kicked, punched
and flailing
I loose hold
to sink into the sea,
only to be sucked lower
by the down pull of the rotten hull.

As I rise, briefly,
the rising sun blinds my salt burnt eyes,
I gasp, one last breath
that contains my whole world now,
and, drained, surrender.

Iconoclasm

When even the ruins tumble
then nothing is sacred for
it is the very sacredness
that carries poison for the iconoclast.

Symbols of the past,
echelons of belief,
bastions of the status quo,
come toppling to the ground.

The old cling tightly to their ways
convinced they are sublime,
supreme,
sacrosanct
While the iconoclast respects nothing,
fears everything
that carries echoes
and embodies the ancient power
hell bent on their destruction
for it is the things,
the symbols,
that provide the glue that sticks,
that holds up the dream, and
unites the people
that they would reduce to impotence.

The new religion must replace the old,
succumb or perish,
is the cry,
we take no prisoners
in this fight for ideological supremacy,

there is no room for co-existence,
winner takes all.

The old have grown soft in their ways,
with their comforts,
complacent that their norms are universal,
common to all, best for everyone.
Arrogance their Trojan Horse,
they stand like Canute
before the incoming tidal wave,
helplessly waving their hands.

What of our good? Our beauty?
Our arts?
If not for us, they wail,
where would you be?
Put it in the attic,
bury it in sand,
leave it hidden
for generations to discover
when it will emerge
devoid of its power,
an empty vessel,
a curiosity only.

This is a fight for survival,
not of people,
but for their souls,
their cherished beliefs,
for what they hold
more dear than life.
You'd better believe it,
for nothing else will save you.

Curled up

Sticks and stones may break ....
curled up in the dark
the urge to spring forth,
to stretch and seek the light
moves in my core, deep in the earth's heart.
Softly, gently, though with an iron will
I lift my head
seeking the cracks and crevices
that will allow access
to the beyond.
Rains' tears, and Suns' smile
feed my hunger
for the Unknown, ever beckoning
realm, till
coming out in violet dress
I make my debutant
curtsy to the world
in thankfulness for this,
my place
squeezed between life's rock
and the eternal hard place
I dance in gentle breeze.

Hearing Summer

The air around is heavy with sound
from the brushing sigh of leaves
on tossing branches
to the insistent trill
of a hungry fledgling
with wings aflutter.
Further away
a cow calls for her calf and
cicada reverberate endlessly
while on high a lark gives praise.
Nearer,
a fly hums persistently around
and twigs scratch the iron roof.

Greed

Gim'me, gim'me, gim'me more,
it doesn't seem to matter what I give
it's never, never, never
going to be enough.

The little hands reach out
and grab my breast, and suckling
drain the white blood life from me,
feasting upon my very vitals,
draining all I am
with unrepentant greed
from one grey dawn's break
until another's chorus.

The young
are greedy, needy, pleading,
for ever more and more
and it doesn't seem to matter
what I give,
it's never, never, never
going to be
enough.

Hedged

Hedgehog, hedgewitch
spirit guide 'twixt worlds
concrete to earth
earth to air
air to spirit
move freely along
silently, secretly,
with barely a rustle
or wrinkle of mind.

Hedgehog with spines,
Hedgewitch with broom,
sweeping the path
clear of dead leaves -
reading the leaves -
like Adam and Eve
to break the spell
of innocence
replace it with modesty
and poison ivy
creating an itch
that begs a return
to the hidden path
where intimacy hides
one with another.

The voice of Love
universally known
universally stilled
out of sight
out of sound
in the dead of night,

creeping the streets
hiding in attics
bought for a farthing
slaving and starving.

Hedgehog - rolled into a ball
covered in clay -
tumbles into the ashes.
Ashes of dreams, ashes of hope,
burnt now to cinders
forgotten and lost
as they crumble to pieces.

Hedgewitch walks
barefoot
over the hot coals
seeking, singing,
steps lightly
safely.

Here we go again

Without some stimulation
or some outward intervention
it's all the same old
same old every day.

Without your conversation
or a little elevation
it's all the same
unchanging once again.

Without some aggravation
or a little tittilation
I'll always be the same me
on repeat.

Without the inspiration
to explore the old frustrations
I'll never get a chance
to change the dance.

Without some irritation
and a dash of desperation
I'll have spent a life of yearning
for a different type of learning.

So, instead of sitting moaning
and continually groaning
I think it's time to make a change or two
- all of which, you'd say, is now quite overdue!

Hibernation

Hibernation of the heart
snuggled in folds of memories
softly pulsating in a dream state
buried deep to survive
the frozen, frosty, greying
as hoar frost creeps across the world
and sunshine fades into a candle's glow

It has been decades wherein the blood
flowed slowly, sluggishly, thickly
taking a whole year to circumnavigate
the edges of a world forgotten
until a touch of fingers, tip to tip,
awoke a flood of expectation
and desire that animate this soul
to a new tingling spring of possibilities
and all my being arose to heed the call.

If only ...

If only I could find a man
someone to complete me,
to love me, to share my life,
then, yes then, I'd be truly happy.

If only I could find a man,
I'd be truly alive and creative,
I'd shine in his eyes,
and then, yes then, I'd never be lonely.

If only I could find the man,
I'd stop this endless searching,
this looking all around outside of me
and then, yes then, I'd know myself.

But time has passed, and I'm alone,
there is no man, no guru, no saint.
and love comes wearing many faces,
and happiness is a dozen surprises.

And now, yes now, I realise
I've become my own best friend,
I'm always there for me,
no matter what I do, or say.

But part of me, will not give up,
it's been so many years, the strong
belief that only if, I find
that other, will I be truly whole.

I stood 2004

I stood this morning
at the apex of my life
and looked around
at what lay both
behind
before.

And i saw markers
laid out
that clearly edged the path
I'd taken.

At first
I thought
they were the flags of love,
lost now
and half forgotten,
but as I looked closer,
I saw they stood
where I had hesitated
on my way for fear.

They marked the crossed roads
and the deviations taken,
so as I looked back
I saw
that though the path was crooked,
though I could have come here
more directly,
still this is where I am.

16:1:2019

It's time
to move on now,
accompanied
by twin fires that
light and mark
each step

I remember ...

I remember a time, a time without fear,
when I was young and could fly,
my memories then spanned the centuries,
and death was only a journey.

I remember, remember a time without fear,
when strangers were interesting stories,
love was as warm as a fire,
and life an exciting adventure.

I remember a time without fear,
when promises were held sacred
and honour as binding as steel
and all who I knew were heroes.

I remember a time without fear,
when the dark of the night
held the twinkle of stars
and the mystery of owls silent flight.

I remember a time without fear,
at least I think I do.
before I learnt of betrayal,
of lies and deceit and their pain.

I remember a time, that time without fear.
but it's gone now.
as have my wings and my heroes,
and the trust, the trust in the dark.

I remember that time without fear,
and I hunger for all that it gave...as I wonder,
I wonder ...

Four Witches

Four witches sit,
glass in hand and stir
the cauldron of their thoughts,
to raise the spirits
of creation.

One, wields her humour,
music and colour,
connecting like to light.

One stirs the darkness,
dredges the past
and offers them
up renewed.

One holds the strings,
and lays the ground,
provides the purpose
blends the gifts.

One, lost and found,
both sacred and profane
sacrifices her art
on the tabernacle of life.

Four witches sit
and gently sip,
the wine blood red -
the crystal shine.
the crackling fire
for humdrums pyre

while,
meanwhile ......
the low hum of their song
grows steady and strong.

Fishing – August 2004

I sit fishing
on the edge of tears
to catch myself.

Sometimes
my impatience russles the grasses
and I dart to safety
under the bank.

Sometimes
my constant clamour
warns me to stay hidden,
at others
the overcast sky threatens.

There are days
when I feel the sun's rays
and the play of light
brings me to the surface,
hungry for your lure,
my own bait.

It's very strange

It's very strange as I look out
and know that the lake
stretches to the hills
with the islands in between,
the mist that shrouds it all
gives glimpses of boats and rocks
and I am left to guess at reality,
imagine I know,
ignore what is truly there.

It's become a metaphor of mind,
grasping at small perceptions
to create a reality.

 I wouldn't want to sail
with such poor landmarks
so why do I live this way?

Now slate grey, storm tossed waters
Draw the eye and
shift the heart to melancholy

I want to stand in the wind and scream,
dance with the invisible partner
a wild tango that sets the heart
throbbing its own crazy beat.

Rain lashes down salty tears
that scour deep runnels in my cheeks
and thunder throbs along my backbone
a macabre staccato demand.

I will embrace the adventure
and defy death,
for now.

Within seconds, the mist has gone,
sunlight streams down,
and the horizon calls.
Thunder still bounces all around.
I am immune.

The mountain tops glisten
with virgin snow
and the water liquid
gold

Last Moments

She said
all my life
I have been too far out
I was not waving
but drowning.

He said
I am no longer here
I have not moved
but here I am no longer

I said
too far out
here but not here
what is this place?

You said
stay by me
ease my pain
it's greater than yours

They said
trust me
believe me
I know

We said
the answers are lies
only the question
matters

I say
alone
unknown
unseen
can I tell pain from bliss?

Then I heard
"There are things known
and there are things unknown
and inbetween lie the doors
to perception"

So at the still point of the turning world,
I join the dance.

*With thanks to Sylvia Plath, Vasko Popa,
Aldous Huxley and T S Eliot.*

Last Night 1996

Last night
between the sheets of dreaming
I took me in my arms
and welcomed you
as someone often known.
I marvelled at your familiarity
and touch.

Now,
as I haunt this pavement cafe,
I look to find you,
have you find me,
and wonder
if we'll recognise each other
or merely sense
a change to passing currents,
as we walk passed.

I feel you near,
yet as I look around,
you are not here, or
if you are,
in this life changed
beyond my sex
and sight
and age
so that I cry out in silence
to the undiscovered future.

Late Autumn

Mist shrouds the bruised and swollen earth
dressed in tattered widow's weeds
where memories of summer's ripeness fade
and promises of grave cold winter lurk
in sun's weak smile.

As daylight moves so swiftly into night
the smell of home fires summon each inside
where candle light and whisky
mark the wake of year's passing
and ease the lingering sorrow.

Life – Now or Hereafter

Do you see a life hereafter?
Do you live in an imagined future?
Do you look for your reward
in some other dimension?
Are you queuing for 75 virgins
with a grenade in one hand and
gelignite strapped to your belly?

Are you suffering nobly,
and rescuing others?
denying your happiness
for some future reward?
Have you existed through life,
forgoing your joy
excusing your pain
for the sake of that gain
or that fame
after death.

Were you promising yourself
that tomorrow you'd change,
tomorrow you'd save
the world from itself,
forgetting to start
with your own crippled heart.

It's so safe to
deny the here and the
now for some future escape
and reward in the sky.
The dolphin exists in its own element

knowing the now
and the how
of its life
without seeking excuses
for failing to swim
or to hunt or
to play
Without seeking excuses
for killing its prey.

Longing

There is a knot
not visible to the eye
I sense inside
sides closing down
down of an eider
either way
weighs little

Looking Over Old Journals

This time it will be different
is the promise i made,
yet looking back
over old journals
I see the same refrains

This time it will be different
my mind decided
yet the emotions
rebelled

This time it will be different
my heart demanded
yet the old mistakes emerged
again

This time it will be different ...
how

This time

This time
browned edges
to the pages
reveal a spider scrawl
smudged
here and here
by undammed tears
this time
as old as first love
lost
sends messages

bottle wrapped
drifting
on the tide of hope
to rocky shores
or silvered surf

This time is
for remembering
recalling
revisiting
still the ache swells
rib tight
as if for the first time
this time

Loss

I cannot say that time will heal
for an amputated limb is never there
I cannot say that you'll forget
for memories will haunt you to the end.

Magic Mirror

I would hold laughter, love and joys
wrapped in a beauteous whole
and wear it like the finest coif
to warm my heart and soul

And, mirror mirror on the wall
I beg of you remove
the aches and pains that cause my fall
when my feet just want to groove.

Mirror on the Wall

Standing in front of this full length magic mirror,
I see my mother!
Hair barely grey,
though with this flattering white streak
in the front *rather proud of that,*
but too long for a woman my age
...la la.
Still I like it that way
as I can put it up,
wash and shake dry,
and not have to waste time
primping ...
and that shows in most things.
No make up
a lie! I had eyeliner tattooed
so I always look a little dressed!
lipstick worn off
I really must get this new stain lipstick,
for I'm too busy to keep painting my face,
and a few wrinkles,
mostly from sun and laughter.
I'm not nearly as pretty as I imagine!
it's always a shock to see a photograph
and to realise how much smaller I've become,
and a little more stooped than I imagine,
and the glasses make me seem like an owl.

Physically,
I hide the aches and pains
of my aging body,
but my tummy bulges
by the end of day

as I relax, and
walking down the stairs
can become a whole new adventure
in navigation!
Luckily
it doesn't show
once everything is oiled
by movement,
and I can still boast of the 10kms
I walked today.

However magic the mirror,
it will not show either my loneliness
or my self reliance,
two sides of the same coin.
It will not show my creativity
or my laziness,
another coin in the bag.
It will show though
that I am proud of who I am
and what I've done,
it shows in my bearing
and in my impatience with drivel.
However, it also shows
the teacher in me
who would see everyone around
rise beyond their own heights
and bask in their reflected glory,
like buttercups held beneath the chin.

Do you want more?

Put on a little perfume
my passion,
find some shoes and
go have dinner with friends!

Memories

The magic swelled between us
as we recalled those treasured moments
that caught in the gossamer threads
of our connection and set to humming
the waft and weft of our plaid
weaving from fragile strands
a blanket that kept us warm
in the coldest of times.

We shared so much
and took delight in teasing out
the strands of memory
to release ever more vibrant
patterns.

Now, I sit alone
and clasp that covering close
as it grows thin and shrinks
unseen
and hunger for the wild elixir
that fed our togetherness.

New Year Resolution

Self help books drive me crazy
full of sanctimonious,
obvious
platitudes.
If it was all as easy as they say
I would have done it years ago
I know exactly what I want to do
that has never been the problem
it isn't that I've never really tried
or wouldn't want to be that perfect me
it's simply that there's glue
that keeps me stuck
repeating over and over
the very thing I never meant to do.
So once again I'll make a list of things
that I'm intent on changing this time round
but in my heart I know
the lethargy will win
unless unless
it's what I really want
then maybe this time something else will change
and all those sticky things will come unstuck.

Nota Bene 2

All around is confusion
only comic heroes for a compass
and for the young
a world full of lies and deceptions,
contradictions and distrust,
so that even their growing sexuality
is suspect.
Loaded with hormones
ingested along with cancer breeding sugars
they follow the social trends
in self mutilation and denial
loosing their identity in a morass of letters.

Yet, there are voices calling,
demanding accountability,
who stand out from the crowd
willing to become the new norm.

Of Trees and Wind

The breeze flicks my hair
this way and that
a gentle nudge and push
from here and there.

But in the tall trees
sun-blessed leaves
crazily twist and turn
brushing against each other
with a deafening sigh,
like the waves on stony beaches,
louder here, then there,
endless notes
that change
from beech to oak,
yet here,
sun-soaked
I'm barely touched
by brief swirls that pass,
rushing to join the crowd,
to find a powerful,
long-limbed tree
and climb the branches,
tossed and turned,
this way and that.

It is a sound of memories,
telling tales of where its been,
whispering of ways to go,
calling   calling   calling
in the most promising of tones
too breathy to understand.

On Dragon Song

I wrote a poem once of dragons
before Danyrs birthed hers,
and after Puff took flight.
I've lost it now,
but the words hover in the twilight of my heart,
guarding the gems of inspiration
that fuelled that song.
I mourn the lost magic of that time,
the miracle of its creation
that I abandoned for a colder world.
It saddens me to know that still born
it can never know the joy of existence.

On Eagle's Wing

Beaten silver in the surf
I would drift through decades
before finding my true place.

Once I was picked up and thrown
for a dog to fetch, before falling back
into the swell.

Once my ends charred in the fire
lit beneath stars, before being swept
back by a spring tide.

Now, I am part of this eagle's wings
I soar into life, freed, unfettered
with new meaning.

On Living too Long

Too many thoughts
rampage through me
chipping at the carapace
I call safe

My hands tingle with memory
hard muscle beneath soft skin
my body screams
silently
I smile and look away
this is not seemly!
at your age!
The agony of deception
not just of you,
but worse,
of self.

Look away,
and my hand moves
to hover unconsciously
over the permitted,
delicious,
sensuous,
substitute.
You call it chocolate
and I?
What's left of Life!

Open Eyes

After a tempestuous night
filled with god's tears,
my eyes opened
to a diamond clear morn,
clear cut
sparkling,
no clouds,
and in the far distance,
looking close enough to touch,
snow on the mountains.

Why do I tell you this?
Maybe, because I have never seen
lingering raindrops
sunlit
kissing the leaves.

Pain

Pain, they say, is a block in the emotions settling in the specific areas of the skeletal body.

But no,

Pain is the dammed up flow of creativity that has no outlet and swells and swells, unseen and un-acknowledged within the heart until it poisons all the intergalactic links within its orbit.

Pain is the scream that has no outlet, turned in upon itself for fear it will offend, whose voice is silenced by a hundred million tiny deniers.

Pain is a luxury to those on the brink of extinction whose very lives are etched in the soil and carved from rocks, it is the constant drone of impossibility that stifles and condemns.

Pain is a cry for change, an alteration of norms, a refusal to accept the intolerable, a benediction from the future to our past self.

Particular

That moment which overwhelms
when the familiar shouts
its unexpected news

It was the seasons change
exploded summer uniformity
into a myriad tones.
For a frozen second
the heart stops
and wonder suffuses
everything with a new dimension
full of story, promise and mystery
when the focus shifts
from seeing the whole
to a sharpened sense of the particular.

Recalling Life's My(ths)

8 find god , be a nun
Live happily ever after

18 find a man, get married,
Live happily ever after.

28 have children, be a mother,
Live happily ever after.

38 need a job, have a life!
Live happily ever after.

48 want grandchildren, spoil them,
Live happily ever after.

58 find an ashram, find myself,
Live happily ever after.

68 need my health, stay fit
Live happily ever after.

78 where's my mind, need to remember.
Lived happily ever after.

they've all come,
And gone,
None of it filled the void for ever.
Only in my giving
Came the gifts
Only in my living
Came life
Only in the crying and the laughing
Was my heart full
Always
Yet I didn't know it then.
I didn't recognise love's guise.

Roundel – Frozen

To follow the call of the frozen land
you left your family and friends
you disappeared with the wave of the hand
though you swore to make amends
To follow the call of the frozen land
you had to face your fears
and leave all comfort far behind and
pack up all your gear.
You left your family and friends
and all alone you went
where ice and snow contend
to force you to lament.
You disappeared with the wave of the hand
and were never seen again,
you're tomb became an ice bound band
around where you were slain.
Though you swore to make amends
there's no future now for us
and all the love was frozen
in your solitary lust
to follow the call.

Sister

Woman moans
hair all wrong
varnish chipped
voice unheard,
less Pay
it's just not fair.

Call me fat, or too thin.
ugly or too fair,
in my world
I shout aloud
it's just not right.

Sister in your life,
you have no voice,
mutilated, raped
and sold in bondage,
hidden away
forgotten, neglected, enslaved.

How can you escape
your hell?
It is not mine you crave,
though I suppose you do.
You, like me,
seek only to be where you are,
but honoured
seen
and loved.

There is Blood on my Hands

There is blood on my hands
I don't remember why
is it because I'm a young woman in the first flush of my
menses
or because in my declining years it has dried
There is blood on my hands, the blood of resistance inflicted
by those who would resist my changes
There is blood on my hands, my blood, and that of a
thousand voiceless beings battered into silence over millennia
in a thousand varied ways.
You know them, you have been both victim and persecutor,
There is blood on my hands and on the hands of all who
rescue perpetuating this cycle
There is blood on me

The Good, The True and The Beautiful

There was a time
maybe
when people sat together
allowing for deep communion
that these three crones
joined in a spiral dance
of love and meaning
turning first this way
then that
to create ...
I could have said
an image or picture,
a story or song,
or even
a deeper understanding
of what is
or wants to be ...
now
they've been separated
claim supremacy
dance alone
and their devotees
lord each over the others
claiming to be the One.

One has always been
three
indivisible
a trinity of being
through which wholeness
emerges.

So I look
to uncover the connection
to expose the tendrils
that link these three
thoughts
that are beauty,
words
that are true
deeds
that are good
so that they
may dance me
into life anew
into a new expression
of us.

Power

It's taken four days alone,
(a glass of wine)
and a dying phone
to finally hear
the voice within.

Thanks be
to the weakness of the cyber world
whose power is limited.

We know what's best for you ...

To track my life
down lanes
of pain and loss
that I had filled
with love and beauty

Heartsore and empty
I stood on the threshold
of my past
ready to step across
into a new forever
I could not see or reason

I showed me
the gold in my past defences
and blessed my cursedness
so that I freely
opened
my heart
and skipped

Now,
I hold all myself
most dear,
precious
tender
full of a power
that will not be contained.

Snap out of it!

Snap out of it
Get out of that rut.
You lie there complaining
moaning and groaning
that life's not so good.
Snap out of it
get out of the rut
you choose how you're living
the moaning and groaning
will bring no relief.
Snap out of it
Get out of that rut
so what if it's hot
how you're living is rot
you are moaning and groaning
about where you're at
but the choices are yours
snap out of it
climb out of that rut
take charge of your life
and the moaning and groaning
will fade with the fight.

Springbok's Last Song

On cloven hoof,
neath sun's hot haze,
o'er dust burned grasses high,
in sheer delight at being alive,
I pronk.

Across the veldt,
into the shade,
with nostrils flared to catch the scent
of death that might be near,
I pause.

From branches high,
above my head,
soundless and sudden slithers the coils
each coil a strangling force,
my fate.

It twists and turns,
crushing ribs,
and wraps its sinuous form in ever tighter loops
of doom that stop my struggling limbs,
I faint.

It's maw is dislocated,
hinged,
to swallow slowly all my form, and
in the darkness of its gut
my life dissolves.

My spirit rises with the moon,
and ghostly form runs swift and free,
away from carnage and of death.
I pronk.

Strandloper

Walk on the edge,
cracks
shoreline,
beach
between earth and sky
land and sea
future and past
life and death
tame and wild
light and dark
sun and wind.

Step lightly
leave words
woven
midst the sea brack
collect impressions
senses
colours
dreams
and weave nets
for stardust
sea spume
seagull feathers.

Suddenly

suddenly
in disturbed land
blood red splotches
along the verge
catch the eye
and stop the heart
for fallen heroes
forgotten memories
recalled to mind.

The Dance

Life is a dance.
The very particles
from which all organisms take their existence
swirling in perpetual movement around each other.
A dance so fast
that the eye
fails to perceive it.
The eye
which is itself composed
of these dancing elements.
How can it see itself?

Matter can neither be created nor destroyed,
and yet the patterns it forms
reshape themselves continuously
through the dance,
so that it seems
forever
new.
From the smallest quark
to the greatest mountain,
this dance is being expressed
at differing speeds.
Sometimes we glimpse a little of it
as it swirls into vision.
The magic synchronicities
that surround us,
the symbiotic relationships,
the magnetic moments as,
seemingly by chance,

two or more are drawn together
to glide, to dip, to spin
around one another
for a brief moment of eternity,
in this fleeting meeting of the eyes,
this touch,
this shared moment
this whole day
or this life.

Endlessly all that we are
dances with the Stars,
and it is this dance that calls to us
to abandon our belief in stasis,
to listen with our hearts
to the deep music within,
and to let the love of the dance
lead us where it will.

Is this just fantasy
or a deep truth?

It is easy to imagine
that we have control,
that we have taken the lead
in this dance
of which we are but a tiny part.
Even that we have some control
over the direction
in which we are enticed to go,
but that is the fantasy.

The whole movement
is both so grand,
and so microscopically perfect
in its apparent randomness,
that even the awkwardness
of our conscious interventions
cannot upset the whole symphony
but we are swept up to a great crescendo
that envelopes
and enlivens the next movement.

Sometimes,
it seems as though nothing changes,
as if we have been left out
of the dance,
to sit like a wallflower
while everyone else seems swept up
in the hurry scurry.
To watch
with longing from the sidelines
unaware of our own dynamic influence
on what is being created.
We are at every level of our being
an integral element of the dance.
Without us there is no being,
there is no dance.

The Old Soldier

He sits, neither young nor old,
frozen between the past and the future,
waiting to arrive at a new present.
His uniform echoes the days of his significance,
of his belonging, his tribe and his identity,
the camouflage chosen to hide his dislocation,
stands out on the city bus, accentuating his otherness.
His greyed hair, no longer short and shaven,
tied back in protest, disheveled and unmilitary.
His stance no longer upright and crisp,
his physique now softened. He sits, still, resigned,
an anachronism and a silent criticism
of all that brought him to this place and
hides his future from him.

A low moan escapes his lips.
Well not exactly a moan, more a deep sigh,
of resignation? Of frustration? An explosion of air
through lips and teeth of which he appears unaware,
despite the shift around him as others become
interested, however briefly, in him.
Is it a signal of some kind?
Has he reached a decision?
His very immobility seems to vibrate
with some inner turmoil,
some inner conflict
for which he has no handbook,
no clear instructions on how to proceed
as he sits,
still and lost to the world.

The Rift

Great shifts
divided,
creating canyons of heat,
separating burnt, arid, dust laden, veldt,
home to pounding feet,
migration barrier,
desperation focuses intent,
while ancient predators .....

watch,

jump blind,

jaws snapping, twisting, twirling,
thrashing, splashing,
hell bent on survival,
crowded together.

Sunset shimmers through settling dust
as memories subside.
Divide.

The Tower

Into the dream,
distorted by time,
drawn ever further
from reality,
I clamber.

Earth and water
compete to erode
man's edifices
to his own glory,
In wonder.

Ever deeper,
lost in fantasy,
we wander
solitary
alone.

The Woman of my Dreams

What is she up to now,
the voices murmur in disapproval
as dressed in lace and silk
I glide out of the cockpit
to take my place
for a wild tango
that dreams are shaped by.

Doesn't she know she's too old?
the voices whisper in shock
as I pack a lipstick
to explore the wilderness
beyond civilisation.

Is that her work?
Surely not.
they mutter as I weave
magic with my words and
summon echoes with my pictures.

Incredible,
inspiring,
and so full of life,
the thoughts come unbidden
as they sink back
into their mundane worlds.
Ah yes!
Life is an adventure,
full of danger and discomfort,
that in the tomb of reminiscence
can be relived forever.

So for now,
I cast aside respectability
and the humdrum
to put on fancy, joy and laughter,
grab experience by its coat tails to
dance through the rest of life.

Time enough for tears and sorrows
when the bones break
and the body crumbles,
and the mind has wandered off
alone.

Water of Life

Tears fall,
dropping down granite cliffs
to soak the tweed,
squeezed out
by an over-flowing heart
that bursts
from ribs too tight
to hold more.

Wind blows
through ivoried pillars
in deep sighs
of desperation
tossing rainbow drops forth
to gather in folds and crevices,
soaking the barren skin
to darkening sheen.

Swelling in volume,
sea bent,
fire quenching,
earth nourishing,
fine sprayed,
the river gathers force
riding rough
over rocks and
twisting,
turning,
forging a new path
from eye to swell.

Time passes,
and gentles
the first tumultuous feelings.

What have we done

Insides churn with disbelief
as eyes leak
and bile rises -
my heart races
where i would not follow
and fingers twitch to grasp,
release;
heaviness sits upon me
and helplessness benumbs;
all around
lies devastation
we've named civilisation.

Where there were myriads of unknown other,
now there are only named few,
where rich diversity flourished,
now straight lines wither,
cankered.

The conversations have been interrupted,
the wealth squandered,
the great protectors felled,
and myopic science
in its longing to unravel
has pared complexity
down to its own shadow
and
with great authority,
named it life.

Such is my ending.

What fits the Crime

Can there ever be
a punishment
that works
to correct the harm done?
Nothing can
turn back the clock
to a time before,
and undo the damage.
When the tornado blows
it counts nothing
of value in its path
but treats all the same
and in the aftermath,
the damage is done,
would you
catch the tornado
by its tail and
imprison it?

Only restitution
can swing
the pendulum back
from revenge
so time and seasons
can allow
gentler winds
to gather the seeds
of healing
and renewal.

What's your poison

Don't drink alone they say, so must I never drink?
Or moved by sensual thoughts forego a gentle exploration to
delight.
Talking to myself is also frowned upon, though no one stops
to listen when I speak.
And cooking for one is such a waste of time with nobody to
marvel at the feast.
If, I go to a movie on my own, they look with pity, and if I stay
home they come with good advice.

They miss the beauty of my lone time, the spirit and
connection of the recluse, who keeps company with the earth
and feels the rhythm of the tides, the swell of stars and the
ache of setting suns, and from an inner harmony, finds peace
and deep communion.

Which would you rather have?

Wild Woman

I am a wild woman,
I run with wolves
to soak up silence.
For me, the wild boar is friend
the chaffinch sings to me
owls silently share their omens
and snakes their offerings.
I know Eve in her garden, alone

I am more at home in the wild,
more at ease with four legs than two,
bodies and gestures say more true
than words to me.

I know the need to hunt, to survive,
to fight to protect,
I play, only in the safety of my own pack,
I am suspicious of the offered hand
whose smell is different than mine.

Yes, I am wild, untamed, alone.
but I am not lonely, for the sky cries with me,
the sun laughs,
and the wind tugs at my hair, invites me to flight.

I am safe in the dark, unseen.
I am safe in the light, which dazzles.
It is only in the shadows, at the edge of vision
that you may glimpse me,
and wonder what that was.

Yes, I am wild woman,
whatever my disguise.
at home with the wolves.

Without Trees

Brittle land,
scorched and dried
by fierce sun and
unfettered winds,
lashed by storms
that scour out deep channels,
lacking roots to bind,
or arms to catch the clouds,
starved of health and
polluted by poisons,
still you seek to succour and
shelter your children
in a timeless ritual
of protection and renewal.

Like sheep,
we flock together,
desperate to find relief
from our own lasciviousness,
beneath towering monuments
to our own greed.

POEMS ON POEMS

take one stone
place it in the centre of your palm
- feel it

And so I asked

And so I asked what is a poem?
Is it the words
that carry rhyme and rhythm
and the distilled thoughts
of others
which stir the blood
to light a slowly burning fuse
that kindles the fire of my existence?

Ah yes, it's that and more.
So what is a poem?

Speak these words aloud
and feel the reverberations
filter through
like music
to awaken some primeval being
within
devoid of artifice
and shallow sophistication.

Words spoken aloud
have potency
beyond their thought companions,
they seek to couple
both familiar and surprising links
and summon daemons
from the deep well of life.

And so I ask again what is a poem?
And it seems to be
many voices condensed,
into an orchestra of thought,
that shaped this poem.

I spoke a poem

I spoke a poem today
travelling alone in the car
without pen or paper
and wrote it with my voice
as I moved
and now it's gone.

I can't remember what I said
but it seemed profound
So now I seek
to find again those words
and wonder where they went
Did they just die
and cease to be or
did they echo out
beyond me
beyond the car
beyond the road
and beyond the country
in which I move
do they continue to reverberate
into another space
like a message in a bottle
cast into the sea
and will they
finally
come to rest
upon another ear?

The memory of that poem
lingers still
without words,

only the music of its form
has left
a deep impression on my spirit.
I spoke a poem today and now it's gone
all that remains is a bone deep longing.

On Being written into Being

Thoughts dance beneath the surface
until caught, drawn into the light
by word string nets
I do not own these lines
fished from the deep
unsummoned

Did I draw them out,
was I drawn in?
What matters!

Poet in Contemplation

Something has changed in the innocent entering into a world of poetry. Thinking to simply be heard, I was deaf to the sounds that would envelope me.

Two months later, and still inciente with promise, enchanted and challenged, I am humbled by the rich world of words, the deep honouring of shared vulnerabilities, the commune of caring.

Is this real, such intimacy over the ether? This caring for a voice heard never seen? As I sit in this village square, the people around fade and those from this other world take on more substance.

Poetry

Poetry
is the conversation
I have when alone
with the universe
in all its dimensions.
It comes
from a deep place within
the door to which
lies in plain sight
beyond this leaf,
that stone,
these longings.
It's a crowded room
with many voices
clamouring
for attention.
If I listen carefully
then the path we take
is always a surprise.

Written down it becomes
the memoire of my travels.

Poetry calls

Poetry

poetry is a condensation of thought
With space for the imagination
To play and to create anew,
a new understanding

Sometimes it is a gentle breeze at other times a hurricane,
that moves the air of complacency.
Sometimes the juices flow at other times it takes a dam to
burst our inertia

Sometimes the Clay is finely worked, at other times it must
be carved from unyielding stone.

But always It takes fire,
the fire of passion in the making,
and in the breaking

She

writer's block
must be a woman
as this addiction
is full of contradictions

come sit by me
though not so close
you stifle me . . .
or now so fare
I feel you distant
and uncaring

she loves to express
all her thoughts and desires
in words
unstoppable like waterfalls
and equally relentless
while embellishing them
to the point of fiction

everything I share with you
comes pouring out
in a torrent of feeling and emotion
that cannot be contained
within the small world of reality

she is insecure
of how her writing
is received
reading and rereading ad nauseam

tell me you like it,
is it good? Are you sure?
Do you really mean this?
You're just being kind.
It's junk, a poor thing I ran off
thoughtlessly.
Let me delete it.
Wait, what of this phrase?

and fearful
of losing words
like her looks
with the passage of time

poetry is my reality, my anchor
in this world and I tremble
in dread and fear that the mind
will wrinkle up and fade
leaving me voiceless

Striving for Inspiration

Striving for inspiration I am blinded by the morning sun of
my yearning.
I remember when Words lit my world like fireflies
I remember when a new image would bring fresh horizons,

And my world Danced.
Now in the harsh light of my days
my words
tumble like pebbles on the beach
battered by the endless waves of the mundane
smoothed and rounded they refuse to balance, and fall heavy
and the locks to creativity have rusted with disuse.

The Fires dimmed
and even the hunger forgotten
until you called.
until you blew on the embers
and with the draught of your
passion
caused tiny sparks to fly.

Summer Heat

Hot,
sleepy,
summer days
orchestral bees and
bird choir
subdued,
cicadas whirring,
endless
and the heat,
damp on the skin,
sun too powerful
for movement
lifts the thick scent of gardenias
to drown the senses.
The soft clink of ice on glass
a promise.
Hot,
burning hot.
hay drying in long ropes
across the fields
waiting for the baler,
everything waits,
waits now.

Even words are sluggish,
slow and laboured
with all emotion
burnt out
by summer's heat.

Synchronised Poems

On the other side
of everything
out of sight
and reach
I feel a tug
on my imagination
that forces me
to its will.

Is it me or you?

Without the least connection
in time
or space
words gush forth
reverberating
between us
creating
their own meaning
goose flesh strong
washing away
the clutter
of predigested thoughts
and springing open
new horizons.

The Other Companion

Sitting
sipping
on the river's edge
with time to kill and
hunger to feed
watching the feet
of passers by
lingering
longing
for something new
to sweep me up and
take the lead.

I could sit here

all alone
all forlorn
all hope gone
blind to the sun
the voices soft
the people all around.

Or own my life
my choice
my gifts and
take this time to revel
in the shimmering light
the haunting thoughts
the poetry that springs
unbidden into this quiet
self place.

Too Many Words

Too many words
swirl like huge rain drops
in a thunderous storm,
bombarding me
until I'm soaked
and shivering cold,
withdrawn
into an inner space
behind imaginary glass
that nothing penetrates.

From here
I listen to the ranting sounds
that hum
a distant lullaby
to drift beyond,
carried on one word
I heard when first drops fell.

When the Muse comes a-knocking

There's a gentle, persistent knocking
at the windows of my heart
that is begging for acceptance and
a chance to make a start.
It's an old friend come to call
that I haven't seen at all
in the months and years that flew passed
while my mind was somewhat parked.

I'm afraid to open up and invite this stranger in
less they think that I have room for them to stay
and no matter what I say,
about how busy I've become
I know that they just will not go away.
So, with one hand on the latch,
(I can hear her drawing near,)
and another on the lock to bar the door,
I am caught between my longing and my fear.

As I sit here in a dither,
undecided what to do,
it slowly dawns upon my fuzzled mind,
that it really doesn't matter
what I think or what I plan,
for this visitor has taken me in hand.

Writing Spaces Poem

The ideas were popping,
there was nothing I could do.
Hands committed to the steering wheel
condemned my thoughts to fly
uncaptured.
But they continued to bubble and pop,
at last, reluctantly,
I reached for my iPhone, then
with one hand on the wheel,
the other fumbling with the app,
was driven to dictate the insistent lines.

This was a death defying feat,
as persistently the poem birthed,
between home and work,
along fast roads
and slow.

Later,
wallowing in satisfaction
at the presence of my muse,
sitting at the kitchen table,
glass of wine to hand
tablet glowing,
I paused.

Nothing!

I tried to summon a thought,
a line.

Nothing!

The harder I searched for inspiration,
the duller I became.

Nothing!

I glanced out the window
to the setting sun,
took wine and moved outside
to be filled with bird songs,
Spring buds,
wisteria scents
and the melancholia
of the dying day,
with my failed muse.

SPIRIT POEMS

slowly spreading circles
touch the edges of unknowing
with each dropped stone

Awareness

Is it possible not to be unaware?
Is it possible to know the space I fill.
To know how it touches yours,
to feel the luminous around
and not resort to snapping it,
to kneel in homage without the selfie?
To pass the sacred without distraction?

Or is my self absorption so great
that nothing else compares.
It's only as I see myself
not in my memory,
but in the digital record of my being
there.

Spare me this, it breaks my heart,
to think that I will truly miss
the beauty and the glory of the moment
because I tried to capture it,
to trap it, this flat facsimile
a substitute, a sacrifice of feeling now,
for some imagined future joy.

Am I fact or fiction

I am a figment of your imagination;
born of stories and aspirations;
forever changing and transforming
my outer garb.

I am a figment of my imagination;
disguised by words and animation
forever breathing and hoping
myself alive.

I am a momentary lapse of concentration,
a blink, a shimmer of the mirage,
half seen, half remembered,
half me, half you.

I am neither this nor that,
neither my past nor my future,
not real nor imagined pluralities,
just I, singular.

I am all of these,
both fact and contradiction,
born of stories and aspirations,
given life by my creation.

A Silent Conversation

Your presence speaks to me
in the silence I create,
its whisper a scream
of mysteries I'm too frozen
in my own mind
to hear.

Ears,
blocked by civilisation's buds,
have grown deaf over the centuries,
disconnected
from imagining
by a sterile god.

It's time
to walk out on myself,
pick blackberries from the briars,
and discover
shy mushrooms
hidden in the woods.

Black Madonna

Black Madonna, what is your message for me?
Walk alone, look and tell what you see.
Black Madonna what is my path?
Open your eyes, open your heart.
Black Madonna, what must I do?
Explore, acknowledge, record
Black Madonna, who am I?
She, she who is witnessing.
Black Madonna, who are my people?
All and none. All and none.
Seek to become the Speaker for the voiceless.

Bubble Girl

Dreams explode from my heart store
like bubbles of iridescent hope,
tickling my skin as they rise into the sunlight.
Stretch – reach - leap,
I strive to catch and hold just one
to bring it close and
keep it near.

The wind of my desperation,
blows them further from my reach,
jump higher - strive harder,
the voice in my head commands.

Laughter,
bursting from the joy of the chase,
washes around these glorious,
luminous
bubbles of fantasy
as one balances,
brief – tickles - teases,
on the tips of my fingers,
another hovers around my head,
each one a possibility,
each one explodes
or fades in the sun's shining.

Time passes,
yet the memory
of those bubble chasing days stays,
and the smile on my lips,

etched with time's chisel,
softens - heart sings
for the joy of chasing dreams
treasures each one.

Close my eyes now,
and drift back to that field,
let my feet lift me in that dance
of innocence
as once more I strive to catch them all.

Backwards or Forwards

when you would slip away from me
I'd like to find a way to bind
despite my strong intent to hold
these obstacles that would defeat
my will to conquer failing hopes
and tackle each that interrupts
these are the little steps I take
when you are here beside me now

Conversation 2006

We have begun to talk,
you and I.

A conversation
that sprang to life
galloping across my mind
to settle
briefly
like a new formed butterfly
trembling for flight.

Slowly
the season swelled
and summer rains
filled the streams of thought
flowing
between flower-rich banks
that garlanded
our understanding.

As autumn bounty,
rich coloured leaves
fell to the ground,
discarded ideas to be burnt,
leaving a lingering sadness
on the air.

Now,
I've withdrawn
behind winter-thick walls,
savouring our seasons

in silence.

Who knows
what we will say
come Spring.

There are no .....

Snippets of conversation
echo

There's laughter
and lightness
that slowly faded
in the glooming

A stickiness
about the buds
of unfolding connection
caused me to let go
and leave
you
standing in water
alone
to open to light
and longer days.

Deep Meditation 2006

As I draw near,
in silence
and in stillness,
i feel you
soaking into me.

My eyes grow heavy
as my mind slows.

A single thought -
drawn out -
leads me deeper

I float
on its echoes
and drift into myself
and beyond,
flipped inside out,
the whole world
now within
and what was small
and secret,
expanded,
limitless
real.

Deception

I saw you stagger down the street
and sniffed my distain
I didn't see the blood draining
from the deep cuts
Life had dealt you

I saw you scream at your young child
and looked askance,
I didn't see the bruises
on your soul
from Life's hard knocks

I saw you sleeping in the gutter,
raised my eyes in disgust,
but didn't see the dis ease
that riddled your mind
after fighting my wars

I saw you laughing hysterically
and shook my head.
I didn't see the tears
that threaten to drown you
each night of your lonely life

I saw you drooling spittle
and turned away disgusted.
I did not see you kicked
and maimed
nor the miracle of your living.

I saw your black shape lurking
and crossed the street in fear

I did not see you rejected,
evicted and exploited
as you struggle to find work.

I saw you dance today
and wondered at your beauty and your ease
and did not see the endless hours
of practice and denial
you gave for this

All this I saw and more, but didn't see.
The pain, the dream,the sheer determination
for my eyes tell their own tale,
create safe lies,
while I'm too busy hiding
my own pain from my sight.

Crone and Druid

HER
Inside this crone slowed, earth bent shade resides full bellied,
clear eyed mother embracing her sky turned, dancing maiden
before the tryptich image of troubadour, Ovates and Druid.

HIM
Come, sing. Sing your song of heartbreak, Goltraì or sooth
the savage, Suantraì, but end with Geantraì in joy, laughter
and happiness lest we forget. You hold our histories.

And you, Ovates, take heed of paths we tread lest we become
entrapped in cul de sacs of our own making. You are the
guardians of our passages, the future seer, guide and
diviner.

Yet to cross paths into the other realms, we seek magician,
sorcerer and mage, Druid led into that other dimension.
Connecting realms we only imagined.

HER
My magic is earth-bound, herb-bound, blood-bound, forged
in fire and pain, enduring, creating, nurturing, continuous. I
speak to the cycle of life and death.

Can I

Sometimes I wonder if I am part of this world.
My rhythms vary from those around me,
I do not feel the same needs ..
Sometimes, Silence speaks to me in a loud shout
while voices babble around me

When I tune in to you, one to one,
my heart breaks at your pain,
I am overwhelmed by you,
enveloped and crushed
lost in the complexity of swirling emotion.

It is in the silence between words
that I find meaning,
it is in the silence in my heart
that I find love,
it is in the silence of the shimmering sun
that I find renewal

In the silence of the seas swelling
that I am cleansed
in the silence of the gentle breeze
that I feel your touch

Can I give myself to that?
or will I seek to avoid the close intimacy
of being alone?

Can I give myself to that?
or will I deny the true love
of being at one?

Can I give myself to that?
or will I always crave confirmation
from another?

Can I give myself to that?
or will my mind continue to question
the simplicity?

Can I give myself to that?
or will my fancied words distort my reality
and harmony?

Can I give myself to that?
Can I let my heart soar with the seagull,
dance over the waves of imagination,
sing from high trees,
flirt with the clouds,
set myself free?

Can I give myself to that?
Can I let go of the past,
the traumas, the sadness,
the longings, the losses,
the meetings and loves,
all that has passed?

Can I give myself to that?
Can I welcome the day, this day,
as a new born, afresh,
not seeking to trap it, enclose it, define it.
eyes open, heart open, standing in awe.

Can I give myself to that?
Can I? Can I relinquish
the need to explain, to limit
the power, the glory, the joy
by understanding it all,
by giving it name?

Can I give myself to that?
Can I? Can I let the tears flow
and not seek a reason, excuse?
Can I bubble with laughter
and not hear the joke?
Can I dance in the moonlight,
when no music plays?
Can I?

Can I give myself to that?
Can I bow down before you
for the goddess I feel,
can I bow down before me
for the goddess within?
Can I bow down for love,
for life as it is,
Can I?

Can I give myself to that?
Can I?

Finding myself

Stop, stay still.
Allow the first flutterings of impatience
to rise and settle.
Stay quiet,
forget the myriad guilty things
you should (or could) be doing
to fade into forgetting.
Be here now,
in this place and space
without the need to fill it
with distractions.
Be bored, for this time,
feel it, welcome it.
What does it say to all
the mindless moments passed?

Into this quietness a small voice
speaks.
A word here, a sentence there,
even, a waterfall of cascading ideas.
Into this quietness, comes self
knowing,
and the possibility of peace.

Without this, life is an endless,
repetitive round of sameness,
punctuated by a few sparks.
I become blind and deaf,
immersed in my own illusion,
believing myself alive,
with nothing created to mark
my passing.

Who cares for all my busyness,
my haste and self-importance?
Who will remember my proud moments,
the task I sweated over, when it is done?
Not even I.

That is not who I am.
in this quietness, alone
yet infinitely connected,
there is a being who seeks
to speak and be heard.
This is who I am
and who I would be remembered for.

I and Thou

Let's talk
about the things
that matter
to you and I
and find a place
to hear
each other's words
resound
with new meaning
fresh carved
from our connection
to each other.

I will hold my thoughts
of thou suspended
so as to let
your heart
guide my understanding
to a new place
and the words
take on a new vibration.

This
I can only do
when fired
by respect
for who you are
that equals
who I think I am
and opens up my ears
to listen deeply
beyond the noise

our voices make
to what the silence
would convey.

When
I can sit beside you
and hear your breath,
and feel your rhythm,
then,
and only then
will I be open to receive
thou.

I Walk Alone

having stood at the fork in the road
so many times
the only compass being
to seek beauty and joy
I have followed lonely paths
into forgotten dells,
lingered awhile
before moving on

each time the horizon was blocked
by a twist in the road
and the signposts eroded by time
so that the choices
were made for a smile,
or to follow a bird's song
or the print of a deer's slots

there can be no going back,
no wishing for what was down the other lane,
so the only regret I'll allow myself,
is that you were not there
to share it.

Life's Marathon

The first few steps
slow and halting
the end a distant dream
far away.
There were times we ran
in tandem
urging each other on
at other times alone
comfortable in the centre
of race, of pack.
Then, a sudden shift,
a surge,
as life flowed into my legs,
the aches and pains
vanished and
the pace quickened
as strides lengthened
covering the ground,
elation in running,
as I flew up hills
passing all
until the tape,
the final bouquet.

Meditation 1

I sit and let silence
descend on me slowly
permeating my being to
fill my core
so there is no more
disturbance,
only deep silence
in the stillness.

Bubbles of love
with source
rise slowly through the silence
enhancing the sense
of deep knowing and
connection.

Moments Away

Moments away from the mundane,
to step aside,
breathe a new air
see with new eyes,
awaken the impossibles
walk new paths,
meet myself anew
where infinite variations
dwell.

So many times
I've acted out
the rituals of my life
performing each step
like a well rehearsed dance.
believing freedom lay
only in the expression.

Take wing, soar, dip and glide
awaken the impossibles
and make them my own.
This is a fresh day
and I will seize
the adventure
.... lightly.

My Road

having stood at the fork in the road
the only compass
beauty and joy
I followed lonely paths
blocked
by a twist in the road
with signposts eroded

there's no going back,
the only regret -
you were not there
to share it.

On Cleaning a Room

It's amazing what a good clear out will do,
cleaning the clutter
and shifting the furniture
seems to be all about the room,
but when it's done,
and you look with pride
at the spaciousness around,
you sense the satisfaction of a job well done.

Slowly, as the days pass,
you realise something else.
Along with all the junk and clutter
has gone an old way of being.
In this new room,
the old you has no place.

It's gradual and humbling,
to feel the old skin shed,
and at first I feel vulnerable
in my sensitive self,
but the choice is then mine
to embrace this new I
or to let the old me reclaim all the space.

On EDL and Attunement 2006

The groom stands
waiting at the door.

Where is the bride?

He turns to walk
along the aisle,
a lonely trek,
from the furthest place.

It is an old, old story,
lived by most,
yet everything
anew.

Will she be here?
Will she be true?

She's here!

They face each other
to recognise themselves
complete,
distinct.

Alone,
together they stand
as one,
talk with two voices
reflecting the same fire.

Each to the other being

the tempering flame,
refining,
two in agreement,
standing against all odds,
expressing
Spirit
newly into Being.

So is the infant born again,
the Christ made Man.

On Meditation

My mind is still,
like the surface of a lake,
when no wind blows.
there are little bubbles
that slowly rise to
consciousness
disturbing the mirror like
reflections
of the world around,
beneath the skin
drift thousands of idle
inspirations
waiting for the hook
of creation
to bring them struggling
and resistant
into the air.
But for now,
all is still,
nothing moves,
and the air is filled
with expectation
and anticipation.
Breathe out,
and gently let the air return
filling the void with life.

A Shared Attunement

There is magic here
that transforms the very stuff
of which we're made
till each particle sings to creation.
and in this place we are
on fire with Love
and everything we touch
though seeming same, is blessed.
is this not magic?
A mother's touch
a lover's glance
and this, a shared attunement.

On Sharing an Attunement

There is magic here
that needs no special props
no witches brew
or whispered incantations

no drumbeat or chanting
no hypnotic dance, or strange behaviours
to change completely
the world I know.

There is magic here
so simple and so pure
that skeptics smile
(for the first time in weeks)

and heavy doubters
walk out with a light step
And troubled hearts
find peace.

There is magic here
that changes water
to wine, each cell
to its remembered perfection

that takes us forward
to who we were designed
to be and clears the air
of disturbed thoughts.

There is magic here
that transforms the very stuff

of which we're made
till each particle sings to creation.

and, in this place we are
on fire with Love
and everything we touch
though seeming same, is blessed.

Is this not magic?
A mother's touch
a lover's glance
and this, a shared attunement.

Preparing to share an attunement

In silence and stillness I pause before the altar of your presence,
feel the earth new beneath my feet, and let my body still,
to breathe deeply the infinite patience of Life,
and let all else matter not to me.
I wait and feel the oil of Truth spread through my mind
bringing tranquillity and ease of single eye, and
releasing all other thoughts, for I am in that place where
none of these things move me.
Only now, can I let Love flow unimpeded through me bringing its blessing
and as my heart swells with gratitude, I realize that
I am that I am.
In this assurance, I step forward, into the vesica pisces,
and cross over into the fire of purification where Love radiates.
Together, in innocence and trust, the fire of love
courses through us filling the wellspring of Life
and we are radiant.
The mind no longer thinks itself, but opens like a flower
to receive perfect Wisdom into its womb and knows that
all is well.
Now there is nothing in the way to stop the power and flow of Love
cascading through, for everything is surrendered into the fire of fusion
and in this instant all is created anew and held for all time,
and this attunement has begun.

Purgatory

Chisel-sharp the blows
that knock and scrape
away the dross
shattering preconceptions
of form
and style
until the final statue
of our being
emerges

Staying Still 2006

"What can I do to return?" you ask.

And my soul
cries out
to stay,
this is my home,
my place,
can I not stay here
always?

You smile,
understanding my simplicity,
as my heart expands
to bursting.

I know I'm not ready
yet
to linger
though in time.
Meanwhile
I sip
from your cup
and every hour
as the clock chimes
I put my lips
afresh
to the rim
until I'm ready
to drink deeply
without being intoxicated.

Step Out

Step outside
the silent screams
for attention that
surround me
in a spaceless,
timeless
place without connections
feel the endless murmurations
of a thousand wing beats
of time
insistently clamouring for notice.

Breathe in
and feel
the fluttering of life
reminding me
that only
in the peace of self awareness
is there hope
for a real existence.

All else is synthesised synthetics.

Stillness

There's a deep silence
that swallows the children's voices
absorbs the splash
cannot be broken

Deep water silence
into which everything sinks
on which the bubbles of sound
burst to instant nothing

It's a peace that flows
beneath the surface
unruffled
untouchable,
and over which sound,
which should bounce,
reverberate,
echo,
falls silent,
cut off,
nothing fades

One moment here, then gone.

Even the church bells
strain to hold the air
yet fall diving deep.

Still Waters

There's a stillness
and a fullness
today.
Images, bright with morning dew,
imprint themselves
and sink into me.
No thoughts churn the waters
of my quiet mind.
Only the reflections linger,
shimmering briefly
before breaking up
into a hundred myriad pieces.
The slight breeze tingles my skin
into awareness,
the sun's warmth loosens the night's stiffness,
and birds call out their joy,
bells summon attention to the hour
but there are no thoughts,
no anguish or concerns,
so, for this brief time
I cannot summon outrage
at the world.
A peace pervades
and I am not sure,
I do not care,
where I begin and end.

The Fan

If I could breathe quietly at the centre of my life then the Wild winds that toss my surroundings into tornado swirls would pass me round.

If I struggle to hold on then I'm dragged to the edge of the vortex, desperately clinging to an imagined safety that takes me further and further from the centre of my being into chaos and frustrations that threaten to hurl me into the maelstrom of despair.

There is no security there.

Only at the heart of quiet breath lies peace that permeates the outer world and stills the frantic poundings of a beleaguered soul.

Take time and let life breathe you back into being.

The Path I Walk

In each of us the wild calls
begging for release
return
respect.

I lift my arms up to the sky
and cry, and cry and cry
aloud to the power that overshadows.

I bend my back to touch the earth,
and moan and moan and moan aloud
for the damage done to her.

I turn to face the north
wind's bite and bow in consternation
Then, turning South
with hands out stretched,
I feel the furnace open.

East is the dawn, haze mired, I greet,
and west, the set, aflamed by man's polluting,
still promising another turn,
another chance to balance and connect.

Slowly, my bared feet begin to stamp,
dust shimmers at each step.
Connecting,
correcting,
collecting,
heart's rhythm into the Earth.
Mindful now, trance like,

I walk the path of life
and on each side,
bidden but unseen,
the grandmothers gather
and waggle their hands
that flutter at the corners of my eyes,
like new leaves
shimmering upon the birch trees.

A gentle "ahhh" escapes like the breeze
and the pace quickens,
gathering me up,
throwing me around,
twisting,
twirling,
yet always,
bringing my feet back,
firmly to the ground.

This is my sacred dance of restitution,
my life is offered for the deeper healing,
consciously stepping forth I raise my arms
to tickle father sky
and sweeping low,
brush mother earth's cheek
then,
turning,
turning,
turning,
turning,
embrace my brothers all.

The Return

The woods are calling to me with a long, deep, inaudible hum
that fills my whole being with the need to escape
to that place where branches sweep low to the ground,
leaves crisp beneath my feet and
twigs create mosaics against the sky.

It's too long since I shut off the music,
turned down the volume of my mind
to allow that persistent call to echo and
thrum through my blood.
It's too long since I last turned my face
to feel soft rain wash away
the city grime on my soul.

Where else can my roots sink back to my beginnings,
but here beneath the sheltering arms of my inspiration.
How else will I learn what it is to endure if not by imitation,
lifting my heart and stretching towards the skies.

Who else would take my neglect,
and lay it out as a feast of welcome,
singing songs of wind, light, air and sunlight
to weave their intricate dance without moving.

Why would I not return to this place in my dreams,
my thoughts and
for my final resting?

The Stillpoint 2004

A physical hunger drives the motor
that lowers the drawbridge
to my own stillpoint.

Tears are the moat I cross.

My constant knocking
masks the gentle click
as the key turns.

I stand waiting.
Impatient
Unaware

When will I stop this clamour
reach out,
gently open the door,
step beyond the known

The Walnut

Instead of lying cracked and broken
open by the hammer of thoughts
with all my feelings shrivelled
and drying in the light,
providing meagre food
for a careless demon.

What if, on first hearing your call
I had dropped to your feet
and rolled into the damp
humus of your presence?

Would i now be lifting my head,
standing tall
opening arms
and singing
as your breath
moves through me?

Unnameable

When you name the unnamable
the unimaginable
the unknowable,
then the myriad faces
become singular,
limited
familiar.

When you talk to me
of your God,
I hear only god.
and wonder that you settle
for such a small g.

You take away the wonder
the glory
the mystery
and replace it with
your image
your father
your mother.

Even the ancients knew better
wiser
when they multiplied their gods
gave them many faces
acknowledged their diversity
devoid of rationality
capricious.

Now you claim god is love
energy

infinite
and still cling to something sentient
knowing
caring
exclusive.

What comforts you
divides us.
Only that which is
inclusive,
always has been,
and can never be destroyed
unites us
in life
in death
is
everything and
no thing.

HAIKU
AND OTHER BRIEF POEMS

pebbles knock against each other
held in the palm of my hand
- chosen moments

August vacation

summer outing
long lines of cars
getting nowhere

Bees and Lavender

lavender flowers
perfume the garden
bees swarm

lavender
clipped hedge
bee less

lavender flowers
sown in bags
sweet dreams

Butterfly

By any name
I emerge
fulfilment

Basho

banana plant
fragile and bountiful ...
inspiration

young man
does as young men ....
hungers for more

sits alone
in inner anguish ...
haiku therapy

restless
seeks a new road
returns

Brexit

slanting sun lit bales
storm clouds gathering over
democracy - brexit

Cobwebs

silk held diamonds
shimmering across sunbeams path -
aspirations flown

Devon Notes

hawthorn
teasel and oak apples
Sloe gin

seagulls laughing
rattle of descending sails
crisp packets rattle

golden road
over the estuary

water reflections
on the hulls of boats
seagulls roosting.

Day's end

drugged on sunlight
high as the proverbial
crashed into bed

Haiku with pivots

snake swims
on hot tar
car swerves

car swerves
on hot tar
snake swims

rain falls
over the forest
bird song

bird song
over the forest
rain falls

Dirt is just matter out of place

two kids
wallowing in mud -
happiness

one mother
clothes to wash -
frustration

two kids
tired from play -
sleepiness

one mother
tired from day -
gratitude

I read the News today

astronaut
in far space -
near sighted

(Astronauts are developing eyesight problems)

a child
grows like a vine -
organic sculpture

*(Children cannot be crafted like carpentry but
must grow like plants in a garden)*

carpenter
designer kids design
farmer

Nota Bene 1

Thoughts
like pinballs
travel grooved roads ricocheting
off old assumptions
seldom escaping
to penetrate new paths

Out of the Mouths of Babes

Is it true that Finland's in the sky?
For when we visit Nonna we must fly.

Owl

Eyes firmly fixed upon your prey,

with
  silent wings stretched
   you descend,
    talons fore,
     no mercy,
      death and
beauty one.

Pari

flowers thrive
wells beckon
Pari ignites

flowers abound
wells are covered
Pari dreams

Pivot Haiku

sunbird
in the fountain
pennies glint

slug crawls
over broad leaves
raindrops slide

tight ball of prickles
under the hedgerow
old leaves gather

Starlings Squabble over Pari

starlings squabble
bells ring out
alarm

new leaves on the grape vine
bushes of sage and rosemary
vino and pasta

hay bales in the field
a saw growls
long summer evenings

old ceramic roofs entwined
distant Olive groves
a dove over tv aerials

cut grass
cherry tree
food for thought

old ruin in shadow
still waters
a swallow's flight

The Bush

sunlight
on the woodland path
that song

jackal
beneath the acacia
insects snore

insects zzzzzzz

The Butterfly Wing

The smallest shift is all it takes to rock the world

within   without

A little tilt a nifty lift and echoes run

from here   to there

A gentle breath will ease the pain where effort fails

for me   for you

The heart's intention quiet attention clears the Path

before   beyond.

Waiting

kite soars
fingers stretch
heart stops

Over the mountains
clouds hover
promises not kept

on a high wire -
a magpie balances
one foot raised

circles spread -
the plop of carp
as mayflies hatch

cicada fill'd days
shaded beneath the fig tree
hammock swings gently

lines of new cut hay
winter's sweet smelling fodder
dance while the sun shines

sycamore seedlings
helicopter travellers
promising new life

relentless sawing
cicada serenade
longing for silence

(legs brushing off flies)

white heat streaks the floor
moving towards bare skin
acid flies persistent

POEMS OF HORSES

so much is said
by those who cannot speak
of love

Taming Wild Horse

She flies free and wild,
mane streaming
in the wind of her own passing,
unbridled
sleek lines of glossy coat
reflecting sun beams,
hooves thunder
on short cropped meadow
and she flies,
leaping the boundaries of her world
to escape into the misty mountains
of future possibilities

He whistles
holding out temptation
on the palm,
and looks keenly after her,
willing her back.

Stepping high,
tail lifted in apprehension,
neck arched,
she circles back .....
only to take flight again.

Still
as the mountains that beckon,
he waits
and curiosity wins,
curiosity and the need
for belonging
bring her back around,

shrill neigh of challenge
echoing off tender ears.

Finally, he turns away,
forlorn she feels abandoned,
unwanted,
and slowly,
head lowered,
moves to rest her head
against his shoulders,
whickering a gentle snuffle
of compliance and
love.

Caress

Feel a shared moment of bliss
as you gently cup your hands
to a favoured horse's muzzle,
feel his warm breath on your palms,
exuding that sweet hay smell,
the gentle whicker of recognition,
the incredible velvet feel
as your thumbs caress
between nostrils, flared to your scent,
the tougher skin close to the lips
and the caress of a wet and
loving tongue.
An oasis of sensation
in which to revel.

Enchantment

There is enchantment in the young foal's eye
enchantment as the clouds flow by
the wind's caress enchanted too
as symphonies of birds can do.

The arms of lovers close entwined
a baby's gurgle in delight
the softly purring cat at ease
the dog who watches from the hearth

A flower whose petals slowly bloom
to welcome bee and butterfly
first bite of summer's fresh picked fruit
exploding on the tongue, enchant

Music that summons memories
smells of remembered youth
the evening light through spring
leaves
and forests after rain

An elder quietly sits in shade
recalling times now gone -
of past loves known -
and left alone
sends blessings to the earth

Freeway

Let me bring you close
to his silken nose
his hay sweet breath
as he nuzzles into your
neck,
raising sensual shivers of
delight.
Run your hand over the
glossy
muscles that ripple beneath
the skin
responding to your touch,
neck arched in ecstasy,
lips aquiver with pleasure.
Feel the power
that gentles to your mind,
eyes molten,
ears tuned to catch the least
sound of your whispered awe.

Let your eyes feast
on his magnificence,
lean into him and
feel his strength,
his love returned
flowing between you,
know his trust.

POEMS INSPIRED BY FRIENDS
AND OTHER PEOPLE

pebbles on the windowsill
lifted from the stream
memories of you

A Butterfly Girl

A tomboy in a tutu!
mud, paint or makeup
colours her world
it's all the same
until its starlight,
rainbows
and cake flour.
Her oyster world
opens to reveal
pearls of humour
splashed with joy.
Luminescent with intent
she climbs the ladder
of impossibilities
conquering my heart.

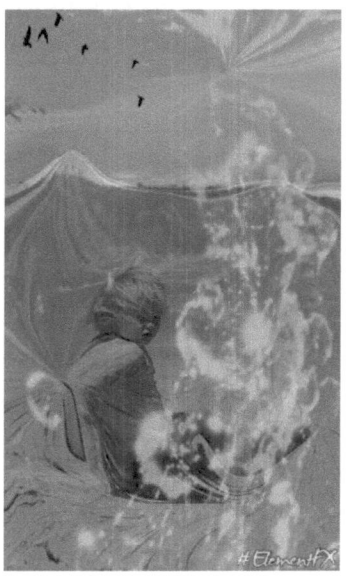

David Whyte 2004

You won't remember me,
though you, I'll not forget.

i mumbled platitudes
as you signed your book
"that the future beckons"
- i bet you say that to all the girls -
or did you sense,
did you know,
that as i stood there
i was carried away?

If you did,
you gave no hint,
why should you?
Your job was done.

You'd hit the side of the drum
with your words
startling all the lazy rodents
from their comfort.

They're running now,
hither and thither,
so my world
will never be the same,
squeaking a new tale
that's yet to be recorded.

I'm scared of the fire that burns.
"It's when the image comes" you said.
I saw it then.

For Ray Jefferies

The surgeon's knife has done his work
cutting away the malignancy
leaving you tired and terribly sore
though glad to be alive.
The surgeon's knife has done his work
while you slept through it all
you woke to see a day of hope
for futures still to be
cutting away the malignancy
has given you new life
a chance to write, and build again
the future of your dreams
Leaving you tired and terribly sore
is the price you have to pay
building your strength and taking self care
are the steps that lead you there.
Though glad to be alive
there's yet much work you need to do,
to build your strength, your hope, your love
now gifted you again by
the surgeon's knife

Happy Birthday Margaret

M ost of all I'm proud to call you friend

A nd bless the day we met some years ago

R emembering the laughter and the fights

G lad that they always found a way

A way to bring us closer to each other

R esponding to our differences

E ach time to overcome the space

T hat lay between.

H ow many times you brightened up my life

A s flowers overflowed from place to vase

P erhaps your over flowing heart was all to blame

P erhaps the generosity you breathe

Y et every day was filled with colour and beauty.

B eauty that to you seemed every day

I found incredible to see and to behold

R iches you had a hundred fold

T hat came directly from your heart

H id den in shyness and respect for others

D elighting in the joy of giving

A nd never at a loss to help another

Y et always full of warmth and love.

In Memorium Jo Cox

I look at a blank piece of paper now,
and ache for the words to share,
words to connect with a life
cut short and blasted into air.

Words to evoke the caring heart,
the helping hand,
the drive for life,
all gone now in a flash,

Words to explain
how a hate so strong
will warp so many lives?

It was words that created a fiction,
a fiction that ranted aloud
turned a loving son
to a murdering bigot?

As I look at this blank piece
of paper,
a symbol now of her life,
a single tear falls
      and spreads
          and
spreads.

In Memory of an Old Flame 2004

How can a lump of lard
fill out my mind
to take up so much
space and time?
Your soggy feelings
swamp me,
make me tired
from swimming
through the treacle of your love.

I crave clean air
blowing through me,
a challenge in the eye,
an invitation to new heights.

Instead, security and mediocrity
come wrapped in false laughter
and a too kind face,
its truth revealed only in reflection
from your children's eyes.

Love's Deception

I fell in love with love
and thought it you.
I couldn't tell the difference
where I stood
though as you moved in closer
I withdrew
to rediscover who I really was
and reawaken that essential self
who drowned within your arms.

I didn't know that I was dreaming
fantasies of love
and conjuring a future without roots
and so I slipped beneath the waves
and panicked when the waters of your love
enveloped me
then like the doomed
I lashed out in my dread
not caring who I hurt.

You see, the pictures that we painted
were so full of life and colour
it was too easy to imagine
walking there
though when I turned to see your face
and the warmth within your eyes
and heard your voice close to my ear
with softly whispered longings
I realised that you were not who I thought
for I'd fallen deep in love with love
with whom you can't compete.

As silence crept into my mind
shouting for space
and creativity had fled
leaving me dried and brittle
I slowly woke to understand
the horror of this myth
for life I thought I'd found with you
was killing me instead.

I tried to find the words to say
to gently ease away
and found the more I left unsaid
the more you moved in close
except there was no me left now
that had walked hand in hand
for I had hidden in plain sight
to save my inner being.

I cannot bear to see your face
with the hurt behind your eyes
and flinch as pain oozes through
the soft tones of your voice
for this was never meant to be like this
the day I fell
in love with love.

Will love forgive me for mistaking you
for I do not think you ever could.

Luna

A welcome wave,
a plea to stop,
hi-five of joy,
a finger's touch,
all these i read
in this first sight
of your emerging self.

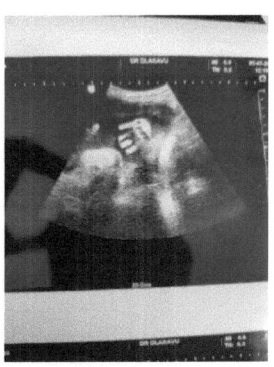

You nestle in between the worlds,
a bridge to what will be,
your spirit self becoming form,
your heart already full.

is your future written now
in palm, or stars,
the numbers or I Ching?
Will you be writing something else,
as yet not even dreamed?

Is that a blessing you bestow,
a reaching for the moon,
a warding,
or a supplication
for love to hold you dear?

In this first greeting, little one,
your presence feels so clear,
that I am overwhelmed with care
for who you will become,
and simply wish for you to know
that I'll be always here.

Marianne

Child of the North,
May flower,
deer like she steps
nimbly through life
midst the tall, shimmering
silver birches of her values,
queen of her domain,
she rules with gentleness,
her love fierce and binding,
her warrior spirit guarding
those she holds dear.

Humour
ruffles the leaves of her heart,
playing a song that everyone hears,
familiar,
only the words remain
on the edge of their knowing,
escaping the mundane,
personal and private.

She shines
with the glow of sun sparkle
on burnished bronze,
a golden warmth,

fires burning in a welcome hearth,
offering a gentle intoxication
to the heart.

Michel, The Gentle Knight

He stands tall,
a warrior in gentle mien,
fierce in his love
and undeterred by

eddies and currents of contention
that flow around him,
a rock of compassion,
and deep understanding,
his sunlit smile warms
to embrace his tribe
protecting and enfolding

all in the strength of his will,
his firm intent.

He stands tall,
and willow like,
bends to the wind,
roots firmly embedded
in the soil of his believing,
his heart sap strong and,
undeterred by gusts and furies,
carries the torch of his creating.

He stands tall,
open handed,
bright of eye,
serious and fierce,
this gentle knight.

Michel 2

Then, as the gentle knight grew older
there came a time when he would test
the values and the morals he'd been taught
and stretching out his hand he tried
to forge a way that was uniquely his
and found the path to be both hard
and rocky in straying from the tried
and true.

Into that dark night of hidden longings
he ventured without clarity of sight
and found himself abandoned and afraid
as stumbling blindly he fell to his knees
upon the stoney road of secret vice
as all about him voices whispered, "come
we will show you what it is to be
a man such as you never could imagine"
and laughed with evil glee.

Each hero must adventure from his hearth
into the unmapped lands that lie around
and taking only what will fit
into an empty haversack, set forth
to find his own unconquered realm
over which he'll rule as King or,
cower as a victim to his whims.
It is his choice.

Ode to Claudius

What does it mean?
And so ....?
Such deep thoughts
obscured in the language of academia,
designed for precision and clarity
confounds and confuses
and looses
the humble man
who throws up his arms
in despair
to continue
along his own
well-worn path
towards oblivion,
destruction,
despair,
not knowing that the signs
foretold
the inevitability of this
without a new,
a broader,
deeper,
all encompassing
expansion into
mind and heart.

On your birthday, Tiger

This day of all is marked for you.

Images and emotions flash through my mind's eye
recalling times we shared that are long gone
and faded at the edges.

You have said your last farewell, and drifted on
to that other place leaving me here
with words half formed and stories unshared
revealing the crack in my heart
which only your smile could ease.

Missing now is the softness around you,
the scent that conjures safety and home,
no matter where I am, the laughter and craziness
that was uniquely yours.

And so, on this your day of beginning,
I lift a glass in salutation and watch the sunlight
flicker off it creating rainbows
that arc from me to you.

Talking about this friend

I

First, I wanted to tell you something bad
about her, though, then you'd judge
her too harshly, so, if
I start with the good, you'll think
I'm only exaggerating
and count it as nothing,
but it's not nothing.
It isn't everything either,
it's a part of the whole of who she is,
the good and the bad, the beauty and
the ugly.
If it was a picture, you'd see it all
in one glance
intuitively understanding
the smallest nuance
of light, colour, form.
If she was music,
you'd put aside your judgement
and let the piece wash through you
slowly exposing the whole.
My poem is linear,
drawn in black on white,
with one thing leading to another,
using words, familiar to us both,
and it is that which shapes your thoughts
to either / or,
to thinking you know
what I mean,
instead of allowing all the contradictions
that make up the reality

of who she is.
So maybe, just maybe,
it's best I say nothing at all,

II

But if nothing won't work for you
do I start with the physical cues?
The sound of her voice,
lilting over the hills
her look and her hair,
lively and burnished
or this smell of her scent
like wisteria blossom and warm bread cooling,
that is so uniquely herself.

Then, should we go deeper
and tease out her joys,
for her horse and her dog;
her fears and successes,
for son and survival;
her loves and her losses
that enclose her heart
stealing her hope
and her faith in herself.

Or, deeper still,
to look at the way
she structures her day
to be full to the brim,
with voices and words

so she's never alone
with herself.

III

Now, I find the last words
linger sad in my heart,
erasing her smile and her warmth
and her fire,
So, maybe, just maybe
It would have been better
If I had said nothing,
nothing at all.

The Call of the Shaaman

You'll think me daft
but I could swear
she walks between the worlds
in thinnest air.

She is not anchored here
like you and I
for she will slowly disappear
a fading cry.

Her gift has thus become her curse
for she will now
not speak for those whose pain is worse
and know not how.

So angry spirits gnaw away
on bone and tissue
taking all her strength to stay
from falling through the fissure.

Her heart which still shines brightly
a guiding star
provides direction to those gone lightly
cross the bar.

For she is called to walk between the worlds
a bridge for others
and in denying this they gnaw
upon her bones and tissues
so that she fades before our eyes.

For she is called by those who will be answered
to speak for them
and in denying this she will be drained
of life's blood
until she speaks what only she can hear.

For she is called to quieten their dis-ease
and bring them peace
and in denying them she will not sleep
or rest in peace
but toss upon the unquiet earth.

For she is called upon by forces we can't know
to translate longings
and in denying this, her own desires
consume her being
to a small spark that burns her up.

For she is called upon to find that path
between the worlds
and in denying that she cannot live
in this
nor will they let her die.

You'll think me mad
I know
and all my rational, 20th-century mind
revolts at this
yet, in my Celtic, druid, earthiness
I feel
this call reverberate cross time
demanding your acceptance.

Tim, Divining Water

You, like a primitive god
stood linking heaven and earth,
arms raised to bless,
lightly held the rods
which summon
the secret power
of fire and water
so as you stepped out your measure
they danced in your hands.

I, feeling your presence,
trembled
at the strength of your summons,
and pregnant with surrender
feared your divining of my mysteries.

This friend ....

The first thing you'll notice in her voice
is the soft Irish lilt hiding in it
mixing music and misty mornings,
soft rain and lots of craic.

You'll notice she moves fast, as though
time is too short for everything
she needs to get finished,
trailing chaos behind her.

There's no doubt in her mind
that she's queen of her world,
demanding attention, needing your homage,
and dispensing largesse.

She'll invite you in and pour
you a drink, then reduce you to stitches
With all of her stories of things that she's done,
and battles she's won.

Beneath her bravado, her loneliness hides,
suckling life from its bottle. Cloaked in veneer,
in plain sight lurk her fears,
glossed over with laughter
and not a few tears.

Time has begun its slow erosion,
And all of her dreams are slowly fading,
She's sinking and sagging under the weight
Of the endless progression of days
Of survival.

She thinks that she stands alone in her pain,
so unable to see all the hands that support her,
she's quick to feel slighted, and angry at fate
That has chosen this path, and now shut the gate.

Caught up in her own mythology,
she mixes high drama with pathos,
so that her voice changes from the music of hope
to acquire the strident, demanding tones of a despair.

To Tiger

17th March 2006
On the passing of my mother

I will never sit
again
holding your feet,
thin now and cold.
It doesn't matter
how much I rub them
they'll never be warm.
How dry they were
and thin the skin
that barely held
you in.

If I could only
roll back the years
by rubbing cream
into these feet I hold,
I'd never let go.

But it's not possible.

Now, as you move
into the fire,
the heat consumes you
and chills my heart.
It doesn't warm your feet
and they remain
a memory
resting in my heart,
small, frozen and fragile

that I could not warm,
no matter how I tried.
Yet, just to hold them
linked your heart to mine
and love flowed
between us,
so the sadness I felt
with your passing
was etched with light
and through my tears
a smile,
a tender caring
warmed us both
for all time.

To Pippa

This child - first born -
of determination
carries life wishes for floundered siblings
light as thistle down
she dances on winds of caring,
serious and creative,
sensitive to the shifts and
currents that wash
through the hearts of those
her arms encircle.

Light
is her footprint on earth's dusty skin,
a spirit child,
favoured with grace and intensity.

A mermaid,
diving deep through
swirling seaweed in
exploration of life's gifts.

Princess of my dreams,
ride free
with wind blown
hair streaming golden
in shimmering waves
of fantasy and delight,
carried through this
realm of care worn strife
to weave a future
diamond clear and bright.

To the Elephant Whisperer

When the elephant lumbered down to the house
she came to repeat a ritual that was now dead.
It could be pure accident,
or simply chance,
though the timing was precise,
both to the hour and the day,
despite a whole year passing.

Of course, that can't really be so,
you made it up,
she must have been looking for water
or just been a habit.
Did you entice her?
Nice story!

The following year,
it happened again,
the matriarch came to the house
and this time she brought the herd,
at 4 o'clock,
on the dot,
of the anniversary of his death.

POEMS FROM MY TRAVELS

stones along the path's edge
mark my footsteps
a story told

Between me and the sea (Barcelona 2019)

Between me
and the sea
of infinite possibilities
sun dappled
gently calling
a siren song
lies the twisted threads
of iron
forged from old habits
and abandoned dreams
knitted together
by cultural taboos
and imagined prohibitions
that control and contain.

If I can
cast off
the shoes
that know only the familiar,
step onto wave washed sand
to create the first imprint,
stride naked
into the brine
and embrace
the first shock
of an unfamiliar element
as it envelopes me,
allow the swell of tides
to tug and pull
so that on emerging,
purified and cleansed
everything is different,

Perhaps
it's time
to scrabble on a board
and let the wind
blow me free
of land and water
so that
all the imagined bonds
are whipped away

then,
on looking back
the fence has lost
its power to contain
and simply marks
a boundary
safely crossed.

I sit here,
sun drenched

and dream
of all the possibilities
so that the fence fades
in significance
to become itself
old and twisted
and realise
the limitations
lie inside and I
was never bound
constrained
by anything
more
than my imaginings.

Blood River

Swift flows the river
swollen
by the rains
providing life all round,
carving deep dongas into
flat plains,
sweeping all before her,
 separating past from
present.

The future arrives -
intent to shape a place for itself -
in lumbering wagons,
spitting fire,
to lager cradled by Ncome
as night falls,
the flickering lights dance
like the spirits of ancestors
flashing an unheeded warning.

Through the mist shrouded night,
bull-like warriors
scramble their way
towards deaths beckoning summons,
seeking recognition of their manhood,
and in the light of day,
finding disgrace and death.

Now, the river flows slower
and swollen
with the bodies of those who fell,

coloured a deep crimson
by the blood of a nation.

The people no longer come
to Ncome for fish,
or the mud
from which they mould their pots.
The reeds stand tall and ungathered
and the cattle no longer drink by her banks.
There are no women
laughing
as they watch their children play.

On the ground, a single owl feather flutters silently.

Caceres

Stone towers
golden in evening light
stand silent and closed
rising over old flagged streets
and winding steps
deserted

pigeons flirt
peregrines hunt
while storks survey

En guarde

Cascais

Look down
upon the mosaic path
whose pattern fools the
eye
into perceiving valleys
and ridges
and slows the step
in wonder at the craft
that laid each stone by
hand.
The invitation is to
linger
and admire.
Time here stands still.

Step aside
down narrow alleyways
and stone steps
onto a tiny beach of fishermen
where houses
blend into the rocks
and iron stairs
descend from upper rooms

to crashing waves.

Look up
and coral skies
reflect in windows
softening
the edges of buildings
that saw the old sailors

leave for a new world
grown old now.

Take time
to sense the heartache
and longing
that filled the women
left to tend the shores.
Their adventure
was to survive,
birth future sailors
and tend the lighthouse flame.

Sit,
glass in hand,
outside
and let all this
infuse your drink.

Walk home
light headed
filled with nostalgia
for a time
you never knew.

Note from Cape Peninsula

As the year closes,
Thoughts of new
and change
crowd in erasing past
accomplishments and prides,
for now the future beckons,
calling on the unknown
unexplored to be met
head on, a new path
forged that will not lead
repetitively back to the same old,
same old.

How would it be
if this time
there could be new?
How would I want
the next phase
of living to shine
in my memories?
What will I want
to remember?
How will I want it
to have been?

At this crux of life,
when many see
only the downhill,
the hills call out to me.
There are fresh heights
I've never glimpsed
whose echo

reverberates
deep in my bones.

Beauty and
mindfulness, the rejuvenation
of loving and being loved.
Courage to explore,
to step back
into the adventure
that is living,
devoid of certainty.

All this I want
wrapped in
the glorious celebration
of my awakened sensuality,
to feel how glorious it is
to be alive,
and how much more intense it is
once the invincibility
of youth has gone,
and the sweet poignancy of time
speeding past
envelopes each moment
in its own crystal,

highlighting
the sacredness
and the profane.

Let me drink long
and deep from that
crystal chalice so that it
may forever be full
and overflowing,
for to leave it
to dry out,
is to wither
and grow bitter,
to crack and splinter
into a thousand million
pieces that pierce the heart
and freeze the very blood
so that it runs thick
and sluggish.

Let me dance
with the autumn leaves
knowing nothing
of the darkness of winter
to come,
but glorying in profusion
and colour,
resisting the gardener's rake,
to rise up and swirl
in the air, free now
to enjoy everything.

On Montserrat ... Arrival

Travelling hot and crushed,
sickness in my gut,
churning, sweating,
why?

When you stand on a mountainside
there are so many layers
to uncover
the birds fly below
and even the clouds become a carpet
from which the solid rocks rise.
The air below is misty,
above clear sky
and sun song.
Close by all is sharp and clear
far is merely hinted
there is an air of expectation.
Will I meet myself
around the next Rock?

Pari 2

The eye is caught by colour
riotous 'gainst stone walls
and climbing steps.

The heart is drawn to wells,
now covered,
holding secret
life's water.

The mind and body feast,
but the ghost cries,
uninvited,
lurking at the edge of perception,
denied validity,
by lip serving, chanting stewards
who cannot discover your name
written in tears.

Salina

The eye is drawn by the heart
away from the hustle and bustle
to the hills and the sky.
Anchored in harbour
the trees call a warning,
the birds scream defiance,
and the wind mocks
as the water sings
its siren song.
Sun kissed
the hill rises high
a promise
a fortress
an ancient destroyer
now sleeping.
Stone Pines entice,
their gnarled and twisted limbs
umbrella'd,
sheltering,
their feet encased
in yellow broom and gorse
climb up the slopes
harsh land
the air fragrant
with lemon and oregano
and I, a visitor,
feel the pull
to sink my roots
into volcanic soil

Short Winter Day

The evening light
of short winter days
varnish the hilltop towns
framed
by Lombardy poplars
with medieval umber

The eyes escape
this world
to wander
cloaked and barefoot
on dusty roads
St Francis trod
looking for sanctuary.

Mornings
blue misty haze
transforms bare trees
to silent sentinels
waiting out the winter tide
while grass crackles
underfoot.

Yet, now
here at midday,
it could be
any time
any where.

Spioenkop

High overhead the lark gives
voice
and from a rock the mocking
chat
echoes the call with harsher
notes,
the wind blows hard across the
scalp
of land where once the fallen
stood
to whisper tales of pain and
fear,
while once again the
thoughtless sun
sucks moisture from the throat and eyes
to render dust those dreams of glory.
A vulture weaves its way above
no longer drawn to barren slopes
where life was long ago surrendered
and only stones, stark white define
the verges of so many paths
that never left this vantage point.
A buzzing fly that pesters now
a lone descendent of the hordes
that once turned black the reddened mass
of those now only known to God
who left the gentler slopes of home
to die exposed on Spioenkop's top.

The Rattling Call of the Blue Crane

The rattling call of the blue crane
challenges the jackals plaintive cries
as the evening sun
paints vivid lines
across the sky and
nesting swallows make their final flights.

In the distance
the slowly browsing kudu
wander through brush and thorn,
half glimpsed.

Distance speaks of promise
and the unknown, of the past
still moving across the plains,
of migrant animals and people
now invisible to the eye.

The ear senses
their voices in the wind,
the thunder of guns and
stamping feet in storms.

The nose twitches
at the smell of rain on earth,
smoke rising from a fire,

The heart hungers
for this wildness now
masquerading as tame.

A giraffe gently wraps its tongue around a sweet thorn branch and eats the leaves.

END PAGES

these stones
placed just so
become stepping stones

Poet in Residence Blog and Press

Poet in Residence is the name of a blog created by Diana Button in 2014 www.poet-in-residence.net – a space for poets' voices who write in English but who live in different countries. The blog is a way of letting voices be heard that otherwise may not be heard and it became a place I could publish some of my poems and send poems out in the world.

At the beginning of 2020 Diana published a collection of her poems in a book entitled *from Pen (elope) with love xxx* through BoD (Books on Demand) and encouraged me to publish mine too.

A further dream or creative idea of hers is to set up a publishing press for poets. Though this is not yet the case, *Stones in the Stream* is a further step in that direction and so you will find the following logo in the front matter of this book:

Below the logo are the names of 4 countries: England, South Africa, Germany and Italy. These countries have been my home during different periods of my life and have played an important role in my writing life.

In publishing this collection of poems I became aware of how many people are shy to put their thoughts on paper. Should you be inspired by anything you have read, then these pages are for you...

Have fun!

Tricia Heriz-Smith

These Pages are for You